THE JOURNEY FROM FEAR TO LOVE

Waking Up and Walking the
"Evolutionary Relationship" Path
With Your Partner

Laurie Cameron

CHICAGO SPECTRUM PRESS
LOUISVILLE, KENTUCKY 40207

Copyright © 2008 by Laurie Cameron

CHICAGO SPECTRUM PRESS
4824 BROWNSBORO CENTER
LOUISVILLE, KENTUCKY 40207
502-899-1919

All rights reserved. Except for appropriate use in critical reviews or works of scholarship, the reproduction or use of this work in any form or by any electronic, mechanical, or other means now known or hereafter invented, including photocopying and recording, and in any information storage and retrieval system, is forbidden without written permission of the author.

Printed in the U.S.A.

10 9 8 7 6 5 4 3 2 1

ISBN: 978-1-58374-179-5

Praise for *The Journey From Fear to Love*

The Journey From Fear To Love provides profound yet simple and practical real-life solutions for creating a successful relationship, as well as wise guidance for everyday living."

—David Steele, MA, LMFT
Founder of Relationship Coaching Institute
Author, *Conscious Dating: Finding the Love of Your Life in Today's World*

"In this small treasure, esteemed author Laurie Cameron provides insightful, specific tools to empower a couple to achieve harmonious intimacy and fulfillment. This entertaining book, informed by Laurie's extensive experience in coaching couples, is an essential instruction manual for successful relationships."

—David Krueger MD, Executive Mentor Coach, author of *Emotional Business: The Meanings and Mastery of Work, Money, and Success*, and *Integrating Body Self And Psychological Self.*

"Laurie Cameron's passion for humanity evolving into the best we can be is powerfully evident in her book, *The Journey from Fear to Love: Waking Up and Walking the "Evolutionary Relationship" Path With Your Partner.* In a practical, hands-on way, she demonstrates how to transform our messages so that we speak our truths from the highest part of ourselves. That is a significant contribution to the evolutionary path in itself. In a relationship, it increases our chances of being heard and responded to with the healing and love that we all desire. Laurie's book is a must read for anyone serious about being at their highest and best in all their relationships."

–Linda A. Marshall, M.Div.
Advanced Clinician in Imago Relationship Therapy,
former Director of Couple's Training and Programs
for the Relationship Coaching Institute

"I believe that books come into our lives at the perfect time. If Laurie's invitation to embrace a Revolutionary Relationship in which you ask your partner, "How can my love support you in living your purpose today?" speaks to *your* heart, then this is the perfect time for you to read this book!"

–Donna DeNomme
Motivational Speaker and
Author of *Turtle Wisdom: Coming Home to Yourself!*
Named Colorado's "Spiritual Health Guru"
by *5280 Magazine* (February, 2006)

"Very thought-provoking with palpable examples of unconscious vs. intentional, clear, and responsible relationships. This book is what we all need to make relationship changes more real and integrated."

–Amy E. Kelsall, Ph.D.
Development Director, Families First Colorado,
and President of PeopleWerks International

Acknowledgments, Kudos And Thank You's

I am profoundly grateful for *absolutely everyone* who has shown up on my own journey from fear to love — no exclusions, no exceptions. And I look forward with curiosity and anticipation to see who is waiting in the wings — waiting for the right time to show up and walk with me for a while along my path. With specific regard to this book and my exponential growth during the process of writing it, I would like to show my love to:

Chet Sisk: Thank you for coming into my life at precisely the right time. The "Quantum Leap Week" that meeting you precipitated was the conception of this project. Thank you for helping me remember who I am — I have been deeply and rapidly transformed by knowing you, and my heart is truly wide open. And thank you for the amazing depth and breadth of Love you're breathing into the Collective Consciousness.

John Thorpe: You provided my first glimpses into and experiences with the true power and joy of an Evolutionary Relationship. Most of the Evolutionary examples in this book have their roots in what you modeled with me. Thanks to your love, insight, wisdom, support and gentleness, I am far less afraid than I was before I met you.

Scott Smith: I love laughing at the weirdness and absurdity of life with you. Your friendship is a great gift that I cherish very deeply.

Tom LaRotonda: Thank you for opening the gates to an amazing community of people that have expanded my consciousness, and will continue to enrich my life in infinite ways. I am truly grateful, blessed, honored and humbled.

Rhonda H., Rhonda D., Donna The Turtle Wisdom Lady, and The Other Laurie Cameron: The Goddesses sure smiled upon me and blessed me when they brought you women into my life.

Joe Mierzwa: Words are my sacrament, and I wouldn't trust the editing of my words to anyone else but you…'nuf said.

Mom, Dad, Rob, Sherri, Ryan, Reanna, Neil, Ric, Janet, Linda, Ted, Boots, & Rick: although we tease about putting the "fun" in dysfunctional, the Driver Family is truly kind, loving and accepting, and I know you will always be there for me when I need you.

And, of course, Amie Campbell: You Are My Sunshine and my greatest teacher. Of all the job titles and descriptions I've had throughout this lifetime, my favorite one always has been and always will be "Amie's Mom."

Contents

INTRODUCTION	9
The Fear-Filled, Unconscious Life	11
The Fear-Filled, Unconscious Relationship	15
Waking Up	17
Choosing Something Different	21
Cycle of Reinforcement	25
The Evolutionary Relationship	29
Traveling the Conscious, Intentional Path	35
Your Declarations of Choice	41
Where Do I Start?	45
The Unconscious Relationship vs. The Evolutionary Relationship	51
Stepping Onto the Path	103
Staying On the Path	109

Now You Know Too Much 113
This IS All About You 117
What About My Partner? 121
Watch Out for the Big BUT 127
Being the Compassionate Observer 131
Are You Peeing in Your Own Pool? 135
Tracking Your Personal Evolution 141
Waking Up, One Choice at a Time 143

ABOUT LAURIE 147
RESOURCES & READING LIST 149

INTRODUCTION

Regardless of whether yours is a traditional marriage, common-law marriage, dating relationship, short- or long-term cohabitation, or a same-sex partnership, this book honors whatever definition of "relationship" you and your partner have agreed upon, and into whatever form of relationship you choose to enter.

Also, the principles discussed here can — and I believe must — apply to all of your relationships. I know that when I began "waking up" after my divorce, it became clear that it was too far out of integrity for me to pick and choose which relationships I would allow to evolve into being more healthy and conscious, and which I would allow to remain stagnant, fear-filled, and unconscious. Some relationships didn't make it through the transition, and I have learned to bless them and let them go as gracefully as possible. Others have definitely taken a lot longer to transform than I thought. They are all still in the process somewhere — and what I have learned from each of them has been worth every ounce of effort, struggle, hardship, frustration and confusion.

Once I stepped onto the intentional path to journey from fear to love and felt the power of my own expanding consciousness, I knew that I could only move forward. I know that my own path toward increasingly more loving, conscious relationships has to include **all** of my relationships.

And if you are currently not in an intimate partnership, and exploring life on your own, this book can still assist you in transforming all of the current relationships in your life, too — with friends, family members, co-workers — even the most critical one: the relationship you have with yourself!

The Fear-Filled, Unconscious Life

Most of us are unconscious. Too many of us trudge through life on emotional autopilot, glad to just get through the day relatively unscathed, hoping that tomorrow won't suck too much.

We are also the cumulative sum of our conditioning — starting many generations before we were born, continuing through our current lives, all the way up to who we are right here, right now, in this very moment.

If we were raised by, grew up with, and hang out with people who were and are unconsciously operating on autopilot, then that's how we are most likely living our lives, too.

Here are some signs we can look for that will indicate we are going through our lives in a less conscious, fear-filled state of Inner Being:

- Our responses are primarily rooted in and motivated by fear — fear of what might happen; fear of what might not happen; fear of not being able to handle what might happen; fear of things changing; fear of things not changing, fear of the unknown, fear of what you know and don't like — just a whole lot of fear going on!

- We do everything within our power to avoid feeling too much (or any) pain, such as from anger, hurt, betrayal, sadness, guilt… or **fear**!

- We find ways to distract ourselves on the outside — such as with medication (prescribed or otherwise), alcohol, work, TV — so we don't have to look inside, out of a deep (you guessed it) **fear** that we may not like what we see in there.

- We assume we have no choice or control over our thoughts, and we blame others for "making us" feel angry, sad, or guilty, or "making us" respond violently toward ourselves or others because we're (yup) **afraid** of taking personal responsibility for our thoughts, words and actions.

○ We desperately hang onto everything that we perceive as feeling good or as having the power to "make us happy," such as a specific desired outcome or event, or validation or acceptance from others, because we're (ta-da!) **afraid** those things might go away.

○And when those things don't happen, or end, or go away, (and they will — because *EVERYTHING* in life is impermanent), we plunge ourselves back into guilt, anger, resentment, blame, victim, sadness, and a host of other unconscious, destructive emotions and responses, including and especially (drum roll) **fear**.

○We spend the majority of our waking hours wishing that our lives were different; wishing that we could catch a break; wishing for something other than the "same old, same old" — but we are unwilling to take any risks or any actions to create what we *do* want instead, because we are (badum-bump) **afraid** of, well, just go back to the first bullet point, then start this cycle all over again.

Far too many of us live our entire lives — from "womb to tomb" — in this fear-filled, unconscious state of Inner Being. And sadly we are, in turn, training our children to live their lives in some form of an unconscious state, too.

The Fear-Filled, Unconscious Relationship

If you are living fearfully, unconsciously, and on autopilot, then your intimate relationship is fear-filled and unconscious, too. You probably live in the same house as your partner, and you most likely function reasonably well together. But if the love in your heart is blocked by an accumulation of fears, and you respond to your partner more from those fears than from love, your relationship with your partner is destined to remain, at best, mediocre.

Sounds pretty bleak, doesn't it? Well, if this is the way you're currently relating to your partner, and you're not taking any action to change it, then it **IS** bleak!

Men are anxious to improve their circumstances, but are unwilling to improve themselves; they therefore remain bound.

— *James Allen*

waking up

Here's the good — no, the **GREAT** news — it doesn't have to be so bleak. You can actually ***choose*** to open your heart and begin "waking up" — starting today. Right now, you can start living your life in a way that is distinctly different from the way you have been living it up to this moment. You can begin living your life today in a way that is more conscious and loving than it was yesterday.

For many of us, we don't start expanding our self-awareness until something really big and significant happens in our lives that shakes us out of our unconscious "sleeping" state. I call it the ***Cosmic 2x4.*** The Universe comes along and knocks us upside the head with it to get our attention and let us know that we're out of integrity with our mission, and that it's time to wake up. If we don't get the message right away or try to ignore it, it keeps showing up, knocking us upside the head over and over again, harder and harder, until we finally stop and pay attention to what we're doing that's not serving our highest good, and start looking for what we might need to change, shift, or alter.

The more drastic versions of the ***Cosmic 2x4*** — such as surviving a near-death experience or a traumatic accident or illness — often cause us to question the very core of our belief system. These kinds of experiences can be powerful catalysts that shove us onto the path of intentional personal development: we decide to review and take stock of our values and our choices, and we ask ourselves if we are placing our focus and attention on the right things.

For many of us, this is the beginning of our search for a new way of relating to the world around us. This is when we notice a longing for a different perspective and attitude — one that will help us find more joy and inner peace. We start wondering if there might be some value in letting go of old attitudes that have held us hostage in that fear-filled place. We ponder the possibility that maybe there's a different destiny for us — something other than being fated to remain stuck, wallowing in mediocrity, misery or despair.

This is when we first sense an inner shift — a willingness to step back and take a fresh look at the world around us. And more importantly, we begin to build the courage to look at the world inside us. We search for unique ways to find purpose and meaning in our work, in our relationships, and in our lives. We experiment with new forms of expressing ourselves — we speak less from our fears and more from the love in our hearts. We discover innovative ways to serve others around us, and thereby serve ourselves at a higher spiritual level.

This is when we begin "waking up."

I want to emphatically suggest to you that ***you do not have to experience a traumatic event, life-threatening disease, or dramatic personal loss to begin "waking up" your life or your relationships.***

The place to begin is to choose one loving thought or word instead of a word or thought that comes from fear. Then make one more choice of love over fear; then another; then another. This is the beginning of your own personal journey from fear to love.

It's been suggested to me more than once that this is too oversimplified. Well, I prefer simple. It's easier than complicated.

> "And the day came when the risk to remain tight in the bud was more painful than the risk it took to bloom."
>
> – Anais Nin

Choosing Something Different

I think it may have been Benjamin Franklin that was credited with my favorite definition of Insanity: ***doing the same thing over and over and expecting different results.*** This happens all the time in an unconscious, fear-filled life. If you continue to respond from fear, then expect to experience more love in your life, well, doesn't that sound just a little insane?

Imagine that you walk up to a brick wall and start banging your head against it. It **really** hurts, but you think that maybe, just maybe, if you keep banging your head against this brick wall, with any luck, it might turn into foam. Silly, right? But this is what we keep doing over and over, only minimally aware that this is a pattern in our relationships and in our lives. We keep banging our heads against the same brick wall, hoping for and expecting different results.

> "Ignorance is not bliss; it's just ignorance."
> – Laurie Cameron

It's not until you stop banging your head and take a step back that you can make a different choice. That is the moment of absolute freedom. In that moment you are finally free to make a different, and hopefully better, choice.

My dear friend, Chet Sisk, an international speaker and teacher, and the author of **Seven Steps to Success I Learned From Homeless People** (Stratford Books, Inc., 2005), has been lovingly teaching a weekly Life Skills class at Samaritan House homeless shelter in Denver,

Colorado, for over five years. One of his consistent and persistent messages to the residents is:

> *The thoughts and choices that got you in here **ARE NOT** the same thoughts and choices that will get you out of here.*

Being homeless is undoubtedly a traumatic experience that can be a significant "wake up call." For many, it's a unique opportunity to reorganize their life-view from an entirely new perspective — one that makes the next leg of their journey more manageable and conscious.

And if you are in a less-than-fully-conscious relationship, the message is **the same** for you:

> *The thoughts and choices that co-created your current fear-filled, unconscious relationship **ARE NOT** the same thoughts and choices that will provide your relationship with the freedom to evolve.*

If you're ready, you **can** begin waking up your relationship **today** by taking an honest look at how your fears have been influencing the ways in which you respond to your partner. If you're willing, you can choose more loving thoughts, words and actions that will likely result in more loving responses from your partner. And if you decide it's worth it to develop the skills, you can begin to consciously create the environment that will allow your relationship to shift away from fear and toward love.

> *"There are only four questions of value in life:*
> *What is sacred?*
> *Of what is the Spirit made?*
> *What is worth living for?*
> *What is worth dying for?*
> *The answer to each is the same — only LOVE."*
>
> — *Johnny Depp* in *Don Juan deMarco*

Cycle of Reinforcement

Your thoughts create feelings. Your feelings influence your attitude. Your attitude is the driving force behind the words you choose. The actions you choose generally match the words you speak. And those actions typically, in turn, reinforce your original thoughts.

It doesn't matter if your thoughts are positive or negative, judgmental or compassionate, the cycle is the same.

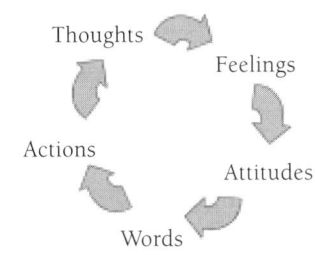

Here's an example:

> Scenario #1 You get home after work and find that your partner has forgotten to make reservations for dinner at the restaurant you wanted to go to. Your first thought is, *"He is so stupid! He can't remember anything!"* This leads to feeling frustrated or angry, which causes your attitude to sour. You tell your partner, *"All I asked for was to go out for a quiet dinner tonight. Can't you get anything right?"* Or perhaps you take the slightly more subtle, but still unconscious, hurtful route: *"I didn't think you'd remember, so I made the reservations myself at lunchtime."* This leads you to not-so-quietly stew and sulk at dinner, blaming your partner for ruining a perfectly good evening. THEN, you bring it back into every argument, every chance you get.

(I have a confession. It was really difficult for me to even type these nasty words. That may sound rather odd to many of you who think it's not that big of a deal. Words like these are spoken in homes every day, all over the world. You may even think that the scenario described above is mild. We have come to think this is normal — but it's not. It hurts us all. And it hurt to type these words — I don't want to feed that level of unconsciousness. I just don't know of another way to get the point across and to show the contrast.)

> So here's Scenario #2 You get home after work and find that your partner has forgotten to make reservations for dinner at the restaurant you wanted to go to. Your first thought is, *"I was really looking forward to eating at this particular restaurant tonight."* You notice your disappointment; you share it with your partner, then say, *"We'll go another time. What are our other options?"* At that point, maybe you choose another restaurant, maybe you order in. You still enjoy spending the time with your partner. The fact that your partner forgot to make the reservations stays in the past, and is never brought up again.

These two scenarios illustrate how one thought can be reinforced by words and actions — with either a hurtful, unconscious outcome, or a compassionate, loving, evolutionary outcome.

> "Kind words can be short and easy to speak, but their echoes are truly endless."
>
> – Mother Theresa

The Evolutionary Relationship

The concept of The Evolutionary Relationship is a revolutionary approach — or maybe I should say *"re-evolutionary!"* It's not just doing things differently, like bringing your partner flowers or setting aside time for a "date night."

Co-creating an Evolutionary Relationship requires you to develop and nurture a different way of BEING in your relationship that allows both you and your partner to consciously and intentionally be on a path of continuous personal growth and development. This is a shift of your inner state of Being that happens on a cellular, and even quantum, level in your body, mind, emotions, and spirit. And it is reinforced with every thought you think, every word you speak, and every action you take.

Let's go back to the brick wall for a minute. Until you are "awake" — fully aware of the impact your negative thoughts, words and actions have on your partner and your relationship — you are powerless to change your relationship for the better, and you will keep banging your head against the same brick wall, hoping your partner and your relationship will change. Making the change is up to **you.**

When you have the courage to step back and take an honest look at how those thoughts, words and actions are draining the Life Force from your relationship, it is in **that** moment that you are free to choose. You can choose new, loving thoughts. And those thoughts can lead to more kind, loving words, which in turn open the door for more supportive and loving actions and responses. These actions then reinforce that new loving thought.

This is how an unconscious, fear-filled relationship can begin evolving into a conscious, loving relationship in which both you and your partner are truly free to grow, develop and thrive.

(Note: The names used in the client stories throughout this book have been changed to honor the confidentiality that is so essential to the integrity of coaching.)

Marjorie

Marjorie hired me because her marriage with Dan was in trouble. In our first session, she spent a lot of time telling me story after story about how inconsistent her husband was, how inconsiderate he was to her and their children, and how he never listened to her when she tried to tell him how he needed to change so their relationship would be better.

All of her focus was on him and what he was or wasn't doing. As I gently kept reminding her that it really wasn't her job to change her husband, and that her job was to change herself, she began stepping back from her brick wall. She realized that the more she badgered her husband, the more he resisted and fought back. As soon as she started looking at ways she could respond differently to Dan, she felt much more empowered. She started asking him what he needed and wanted. Gradually, she came to more easily accept his decisions to occasionally spend time on his own rather than with her and their children. Then he also started to respond differently — more positively — to her. She started to believe that change was actually possible. The brick wall — their power struggles — began to erode. Their communication began to improve, and they enjoyed spending more time in a healthier, more conscious relationship with each other.

The Evolutionary Relationship is one in which you and your partner consciously and intentionally choose thoughts, words and actions motivated by love over those motivated by fear as frequently as you can. And this process can, with time, be one that happens with progressively less effort and with more grace and ease.

> We are what we repeatedly do; excellence, therefore, is not an act but a habit."
>
> – Aristotle

Traveling the Conscious, Intentional Path

When you travel the conscious, intentional path from fear to love, there is no final destination. I don't believe there's a point at which you can say, *"I have arrived, and I have no fears left!"* It may be possible somewhere, somehow, but I haven't yet seen anyone who was able to go to sleep one day filled with fear and wake up the next day with all their fears having dissipated overnight.

For the majority of us humans, it is a process that happens over time. I think it's more likely that we learn how to manage and respond to our fears in ways that diminish the influence they have on our decisions, and support us to build our courage and confidence.

> "Courage is resistance to fear, mastery of fear — not absence of fear."
>
> — *Mark Twain*

It is the ***experience*** of personal evolution along the continuum from fear to love that is the goal of this path. It is the cumulative, moment-by-moment choices you make that determine whether your journey is less conscious or more conscious.

Think of a horizontal time line — much like those that chronicle the history of anything:

```
--—|————|————|—-——|————|——
A Long   A Little   Present Time   Predicted Future
 Time     While
 Ago      Ago
```

The time line for an Evolutionary Relationship looks like this.

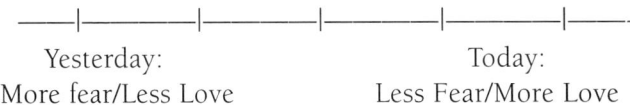

"Success" and "failure" do not exist on this path. The passage is along the soul's journey from less love to more love. There **will** be moments or days when your choices may not quite reflect the conscious love and support you want them to. There **will** be days when you will feel that your fears have mutinied and regained control of your peaceful ship.

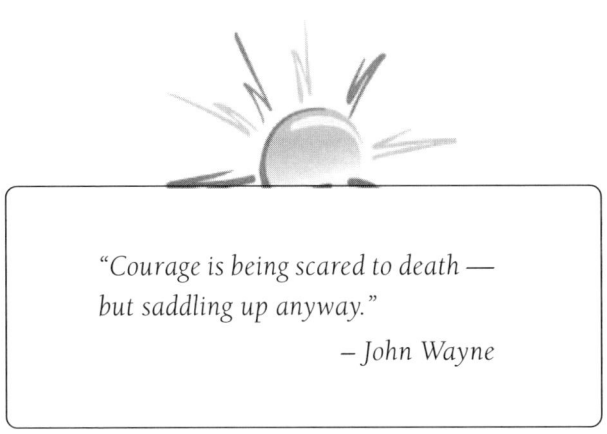

*"Courage is being scared to death —
but saddling up anyway."*

– John Wayne

But rather than beating yourself up by saying things like, *I screwed up; I'm no good at this; I'm such a terrible person; I've failed; I'm going backwards; I'll never get there;* instead consider saying to yourself and to your partner things such as:

> *"Wow! That sure was some old stuff that came up just now!"*
>
> *"How can I respond in a more conscious and loving way next time this old stuff comes up?"*
>
> *"WHOA! Where did THAT come from?"*
>
> *"I'm sorry, that's not how I want to be with you."*
>
> *"I appreciate the opportunity to grow from this experience."*

It's important to learn how to accept each moment as it unfolds, take responsibility for your actions if they come from fear, learn from the experience, then leave it right there on your path — in the past — and walk away from it. Trust that you will, over time, travel in an overall forward motion, expanding your consciousness, and moving away from fear and toward more Love.

The Journey from Fear to Love

> *"Our power does not lie in our ability to remake the world, but rather in our ability to remake ourselves."*
>
> *–Gandhi*

In addition, your experience will be much more enjoyable if you accept that the journey along this path is rarely a consistent one. There might be days, weeks, months, or perhaps even years, when you feel like you're drifting aimlessly, confused about which direction to go. There will be other times when your clarity astounds you and you make "quantum leaps" forward. I freely admit that I regularly experience these extremes, and pretty much everything in between — sometimes in the span of just one hour! What a fascinating roller coaster!

Remember that old saying — was it from the '70s? "Go with the flow, Man!" It's good advice here. Expecting consistency from a human experience is a surefire way to make you more than just a little crazy. Remember that brick wall?

The Journey from Fear to Love

Your Declarations of Choice

Consciously co-creating an Evolutionary Relationship with your partner can only be accomplished when you are ready to honestly and sincerely make the following two declarations:

> #1. *"I always have a choice in what I think and say"*; and
>
> #2. *"My first choice is always to choose Love."*

If you don't believe you can choose to change your thoughts, words and actions, then you won't be able to.

Laurie Cameron

> "Whether you believe you can or you can't, you're right."
>
> – Henry Ford

Henry Ford was right. You really do have a choice about which thoughts you think, which words you speak, and which actions you take — ***every single time.***

And making the choice to always choose love does not have to be a monumental, trumpets blaring, fireworks popping, earth shattering event. Start small. Start with creating the intention to be less fearful and more loving today than you were yesterday. And if that still feels too big, then choose a little more love in the very next moment than you chose in the moment that just passed. It doesn't matter how large or small your choice feels — just make it. And be sure that you focus on the loving choices that you ***can*** make.

Becky

Becky was a coaching client who came to me several years ago wanting to find a life partner. Actually, she wanted me to, in her words, "fix her" because she wanted to feel "more together." She thought this would make her more attractive to a potential partner. Luckily, that's not a coach's job — to "fix" a client. Through our work together, she realized that she had never felt she had a choice in *anything*: her work, her partners, her friends. She felt controlled by her conditioning — the messages she heard growing up that she never took the time to question.

Her coaching sessions were filled with *"I can't,"* or *"I don't have a choice."* Every time she mentioned not having a choice about some aspect of her life, I would respond, *"Okay, if you don't have a choice about that, what **do** you have a choice about?"* Or I would ask, *"If you can't have (or do) that, what **can** you have (or do)?"*

Eventually, she got it — there were lots of things in her life that she really didn't have a choice about, such as what other people say or do, and things that she may not be able to have or do, but there were also lots of options that she **could** choose, things she **could** have and things she **could** do. For the rest of the time we worked together, her focus was on the choices she **did** have rather than being resentful and angry about the choices she ***didn't*** have. She rapidly grew more confident, and found more joy in every area of her life. She let go of feeling that she needed to be "fixed," and she finally saw herself as "just right." Last I heard from her, she was traveling like she'd always wanted to, and she was starting her own business. She was able to create some very positive momentum in her life when she finally accepted that she always had options, and that it was much more productive to focus on the choices she ***did*** have, rather than on the ones she ***didn't*** have.

Where Do I Start?

The best place to begin is with knowing what perpetuates an "unconscious" state of inner Being in a relationship, the thoughts, words and responses that are rooted in fear and drain your Life Force energy. You can recognize this state of Being in yourself when you feel small, powerless or withdrawn; when it feels like you're shrinking back into yourself. The outward expression of this state of Being is typically either withdrawing from your partner or acting in an aggressive, defensive manner toward your partner.

In contrast, then, you need to know what constitutes an "evolutionary" state of inner Being in a relationship.

The intentional selection of those thoughts, words and actions that allows you and your partner the freedom to more gracefully evolve into a higher, expanded consciousness, both individually and collectively.

In the next section of this book I share some "Unconscious" and "Evolutionary" relationship distinctions. I offer examples of what you might think, feel, say, or do if you are in a place of fear, and contrast that with what you might think, feel, say or do when you choose love in a similar situation.

This list is certainly not exhaustive. And because we are a species of infinite diversity, there are an infinite number of possible variations for each of the examples described. My intention has been to describe Unconscious Relationship scenarios that are somewhat universal in their essence — the words may be different for different people, but the fears behind the words feel pretty common. We can probably all recognize these examples either in our own relationships or in some of the relationships we've observed throughout our lives.

The "Evolutionary Relationship" responses are suggestions — they come from my own experiences, and the style of language is definitely mine. Your responses will likely be different because they will come from your own heart, in your own words. Use each description offered as a springboard for your own creativity, and to develop your own style with your partner.

As I have already suggested, this is not a process that you can expect to happen quickly. Just as the evolutionary path of the human species has happened over the last 60 million years — give or take a few millennia — your own path of personal evolution is also one that has progressed and will continue to progress gradually over your lifetime. I cannot say how it will unfold for you. That mystery is a gift that only you can receive and open.

As you read these, I invite you to be open and willing to experiment, to push your envelope, and to take some risks in order to take that next step along the path of your own expanded consciousness.

"Try on" the Evolutionary Relationship suggestions to see how they fit your style. Step into possibility thinking and ask yourself, *"What thought can I choose right now that will create an expanded sense of love and inner peace in this situation?"*

And definitely feel free to add your own "Unconscious" and "Evolutionary" relationship distinctions as

you begin to more closely observe yourself, your partner, and the people around you and how they are Being in their relationships.

My intention is to offer these basic distinctions as a mirror. If you see yourself in one of the Evolutionary Relationship descriptions, congratulations! That means you're waking up, and you and your partner are creating love and joy in your relationship.

If you see yourself in one of the Unconscious Relationship descriptions, congratulations! That means you have the courage to be honest with yourself, and you are now free to make a different choice. Suspend all judgments and self-recrimination, and use the contrast of the Evolutionary Relationship description as inspiration for your own shift from fear to love.

If you see your partner in one of the "Evolutionary Relationship" descriptions, call her right now and say *"THANK YOU!"*

And if you see your partner in one of the "Unconscious Relationship" descriptions, bless him with compassion, and trust the he is right where he needs to be on his own path.

Also, below each pair of distinctions is a line that represents the continuum from fear on one extreme, to love on the other extreme. I invite you to place an "x" on the line that represents where you feel you are *TODAY* along the path from fear to love. Being honest with yourself keeps you on the Evolutionary path; "fudging" your answer is less-than-conscious.

And consider putting a date above each "x" too. That way, you can come back to these distinctions in the future and use today's assessment as a way to track your progress on your path. If you choose to do this, you can actually track your own personal evolution — your own journey from fear to love.

EXAMPLE:

Where I am today between fear and love:

(4-24-08)
FEAR |————————————-**x**————————| LOVE

Are you ready to jump on the path? Let's get going!

The Unconscious Relationship vs. The Evolutionary Relationship

Very Important Note: In the following examples, I use the masculine and feminine interchangeably to avoid the cumbersome repetition of his/hers, he/she, or him/her. I am in **no way** implying that either men or women are any more or less conscious than the other gender. Just as an "Evolutionary Relationship" is equally accessible to both men and women, it is also true that "Unconscious" is an equal opportunity affliction. So please **DO NOT** use my choice to simplify the readability by saying either "him" or "her" as a justification to "genderalize" any of the unconscious or evolutionary behaviors described below! THANK YOU!

In the Unconscious Relationship

It's accepted that some sacrifice of your dream in order to be with your partner is just part of the deal — you put the relationship first, above your soul's mission. Eventually you reconcile with your feelings of regret for having "settled" for less than reaching your highest potential along your Life Path.

Where I am today between fear and love:

FEAR

The Journey from Fear to Love

In the Evolutionary Relationship

Each partner's mission and purpose for being here is at the top of the relationship's priorities list. You keep your sights on your own soul's mission, and you find ways to help your partner clear the path for living her mission and purpose, too.

LOVE

In the Unconscious Relationship

If you choose to sacrifice your dream or compromise your own purpose, you blame your partner or the relationship. Your resentment builds, and is expressed in a variety of hurtful, destructive, and unconscious ways.

Where I am today between fear and love:

FEAR

The Journey from Fear to Love

In the Evolutionary Relationship

If you have compromised your purpose or mission, you take responsibility for your own choice. And you do whatever is required to reconnect with your soul's mission.

LOVE

In the Unconscious Relationship

You start each day telling your partner what you need from her and when you need it.

Where I am today between fear and love:

FEAR ⊢────────────────────────────────┤

The Journey from Fear to Love

In the Evolutionary Relationship

You start each day by asking your partner, *"How can my love support you in living your purpose today?"*

_____ *LOVE*

In the Unconscious Relationship

You expect your partner to live up to who you need him to be. And when he ends up being who *he* needs to be, you feel let down, betrayed, and disappointed: *"You're not the person I married."* Then you bail out and head out on another futile search for that elusive "someone else" who might be able to meet your needs and live up to your expectations.

Where I am today between fear and love:

FEAR

In the Evolutionary Relationship

You have two expectations of your relationship: 1. You expect to learn new things about who you are and how to better fulfill your soul's mission; and 2. You expect to deepen your understanding of the world by seeing it through your partner's eyes and heart. You are never let down.

―――――――――――――――――――――――――――――――― *LOVE*

In the Unconscious Relationship

You feel that you are incomplete without your partner: *"My better half;" "You complete me;" "Two halves make a whole."*

Where I am today between fear and love:

FEAR |————————————————————————————|

In the Evolutionary Relationship

Both you and your partner are whole and complete before you come together. And as you wake up and walk the evolutionary relationship path together, you become a more expanded, more conscious expression of who you already are.

LOVE
►─────────────────────────────────────┥

In the Unconscious Relationship

You focus on everything about your partner that seems different, odd, or annoying. And you tell her how she's different or odd, and what annoys you.

Where I am today between fear and love:

FEAR ⊢──

In the Evolutionary Relationship

"Different" is merely a neutral observation — you make no judgments about any of your partner's qualities that are different from your own. You focus your thoughts, words and actions on the strengths, attributes and qualities that you love, admire, and appreciate in your partner. You regularly and consistently tell your partner what you appreciate about him. You reflect back to him your observations of his personal growth and evolution.

———————————————————————— *LOVE*

In the Unconscious Relationship

You tell him when he pushes your buttons, and then tell him how he can fix himself — you expect **him** to change.

Where I am today between fear and love:

FEAR ―――――――――――――――――――――――

In the Evolutionary Relationship

You know that when your buttons are being pushed it's just a mirror — it's about you, what you need to look at, and what you need to change about yourself.

LOVE

In the Unconscious Relationship

If you screw up, you either make excuses, blame your partner, (or someone or something — anything else outside of yourself) and avoid taking responsibility: *"I wouldn't have yelled if you hadn't made me angry."* Or you apologize profusely, hoping to barter her forgiveness with treats, trinkets or self-imposed slave-like duties: *"Please tell me how I can make it up to you, I'll do anything."*

Where I am today between fear and love:

FEAR

In the Evolutionary Relationship

If you step out of integrity with your partner, you're honest with your partner and yourself about it. You own it. You apologize for it. And then you let it go, because your partner has let it go, too. And you're more deliberate and mindful about staying in integrity more consistently.

LOVE

In the Unconscious Relationship

If your partner screws up, you milk her guilt to your advantage. You hang on to the mistake and retrieve it in every discussion or argument where you feel you could gain the advantage by milking her guilt some more.

Where I am today between fear and love:

FEAR |————————————————————————————|

The Journey from Fear to Love

In the Evolutionary Relationship

If your partner screws up, you create a safe space for him to step back into integrity. The event then becomes part of the past and stays there.

LOVE

In the Unconscious Relationship

You tease your partner in ways that highlight her insecurities or vulnerabilities, and then you dismiss it with: *"It's just a joke."*

Where I am today between fear and love:

FEAR |──|

The Journey from Fear to Love

In the Evolutionary Relationship

Jokes are *never* at the expense of your partner — or any other human being, for that matter. If you do cross that line, you know it immediately, you own it, you apologize, and you move on.

LOVE

In the Unconscious Relationship

You feel jealous or inferior — or both — when your partner achieves any level of success that you perceive as higher than your own.

Where I am today between fear and love:

FEAR ⊢──┤

The Journey from Fear to Love

In the Evolutionary Relationship

You revel in all of your partner's successes, and celebrate with her honestly and enthusiastically.

―――――――――――――――――――――――――――――――― *LOVE*

Laurie Cameron

In the Unconscious Relationship

You put your partner down and diminish his intelligence so you can feel smarter.

Where I am today between fear and love:

FEAR |——————————————————————————

The Journey from Fear to Love

In the Evolutionary Relationship

You and your partner dance gracefully between being student and teacher with each other, and you accept that each of you will grow and evolve at your own pace.

LOVE
⊢

In the Unconscious Relationship

You make up stories about what you think your partner is feeling, thinking, not feeling, or not thinking — and you believe your own stories. You respond to your partner from the assumptions you make, without ever checking in with her to see if they're accurate or not.

Where I am today between fear and love:

FEAR

In the Evolutionary Relationship

When you make assumptions (which we all do), you're aware of it and you own it: *"The story I'm making up about this is..."* Then you check in with your partner and have a conversation with him to find out what he is **really** thinking and feeling — and he tells you.

LOVE

In the Unconscious Relationship

You take much of what your partner says and does personally and assume everything your partner says or feels — especially the negative stuff — is about you.

Where I am today between fear and love:

FEAR

The Journey from Fear to Love

In the Evolutionary Relationship

You don't take anything your partner says or does personally. You understand and accept that her stuff is about her, and that your stuff is about you. You are able to have an open and direct conversation with her about anything and everything that's bothering either one of you. You treat everything your partner feels and says as valid.

LOST

LOVE

In the Unconscious Relationship

When your partner tells you she doesn't want to do something, or is uncomfortable with your suggestion or idea, you try to talk her into it by using guilt, begging, bargaining, or you persist until she gets tired of standing up for her values and just gives in.

Where I am today between fear and love:

FEAR |————————————————————————————

The Journey from Fear to Love

In the Evolutionary Relationship

When you partner tells you she doesn't want to do something, or is uncomfortable with your suggestion or idea, your first and only response is, *"Okay."*

LOVE

In the Unconscious Relationship

When your partner asks *you* to do something that you really do not want to do, or feel uncomfortable doing, you either agree to do it out of fear that it will create a conflict if you don't, then feel resentful that she "made you do it;" or you become angry that he asked, incensed because you think, *"He should know me well enough by now that he shouldn't even have asked."*

Where I am today between fear and love:

FEAR |————————————————————————————|

In the Evolutionary Relationship

When your partner asks you to do something that you really do not want to do, or feel uncomfortable doing, you respond honestly, *"That doesn't really work for me."* And you trust that she will respect your boundary graciously.

LOVE

In the Unconscious Relationship

Relationship success is fundamentally a black-and-white concept. If you stay with your partner *"till death us do part,"* your relationship is a success — regardless of the quality of the relationship. If you and your partner part ways for any reason, you brand your relationship a failure. And it's likely that you carry that failure "baggage" into future relationships.

Where I am today between fear and love:

FEAR ├──┤

The Journey from Fear to Love

In the Evolutionary Relationship

Your relationship is a success if you and your partner learn something new about yourselves, and if you make more powerful and conscious relationship decisions today than you did yesterday — regardless of how long you are together.

LOVE

Laurie Cameron

In the Unconscious Relationship

You believe you can fall "out of love" with your partner. And if you think you have, you use that to justify ending the relationship. The phrase, *"I love you, but I'm not IN love with you,"* makes sense to you.

Where I am today between fear and love:

FEAR

The Journey from Fear to Love

In the Evolutionary Relationship

Your love for your partner is constant, solid, and unwavering. You flow easily through a variety of levels of connection, disconnection and reconnection. You intentionally look for new ways to deepen and express your love for each other. And if your paths diverge, your love remains constant and unconditional — it is never dependent on whether or not you're together.

LOVE

In the Unconscious Relationship

You live each day in fear that your partner might leave you, and in desperation you do everything you can to hold onto her.

Where I am today between fear and love:

FEAR
|———|

In the Evolutionary Relationship

You live each moment ready and willing to unconditionally bless your partner on his path — regardless of whether that path continues to include you or not.

LOVE

In the Unconscious Relationship

If your partner *does* choose a different path, you are devastated, heartbroken, and mourn the death of "what might have been."

Where I am today between fear and love:

FEAR

In the Evolutionary Relationship

If your partner decides her mission can be better fulfilled in a different place or in a different way, you acknowledge and accept any sadness or grief you might feel (because we *are* human, after all). You celebrate what you created and how you grew while you were together. You celebrate the magnificent gifts you each received from being with the other.

LOVE

In the Unconscious Relationship

If the romantic relationship with your partner ends, you view it as "breaking up." And you find ways to *"get over it and get on with my life."*

Where I am today between fear and love:

FEAR
┠───┨

The Journey from Fear to Love

In the Evolutionary Relationship

If you and your partner choose different paths, you see it as an ending *and* as a beginning. You find ways to successfully and gracefully "remodel" your relationship into the form that will continue to serve the highest good for both of you.

LOVE

In the Unconscious Relationship

The "US" is a melding of two scared souls, huddled together trying to hold the unknown future at bay.

Where I am today between fear and love:

FEAR

In the Evolutionary Relationship

The "US" is a sacred space for you to recharge and re-energize your soul's purpose. The "US" is a safe sanctuary in which to spend the dark nights of your soul, so you can emerge with more clarity, confidence and joy.

LOVE

Laurie Cameron

In the Unconscious Relationship

At the end of the day, you ask your partner, *"Do you still love me?"*

Where I am today between fear and love:

FEAR
|—————————————————————————————|

The Journey from Fear to Love

In the Evolutionary Relationship

At the end of the day, you ask your partner, *"How did you grow today?"*

———————————————————————— *LOVE*

In the Unconscious Relationship

After spending time away from your partner, you greet him with, *"It's about time, whadja you bring me?"*

Where I am today between fear and love:

FEAR

In the Evolutionary Relationship

Regardless of whether you're away from your partner for an hour or a year, or whether you have been a mile apart or a continent apart, your partner is never out of your heart. Whenever you come back together, your greeting is always the same, *"Welcome home, I've been waiting for you."*

LOVE

In the Unconscious Relationship

You ask of your partner: *"Please love me," "please pay attention to me," "please accept me," "please take care of me."*

Where I am today between fear and love:

FEAR |—————————————————————————

The Journey from Fear to Love

In the Evolutionary Relationship

You ask only one thing of your partner: *"Please help me remember who I am."*

                                                              LOVE

So, how'd you do? Were you surprised to realize that you were closer to Love than you thought you might be? Did you see yourself more in the Evolutionary Relationship descriptions than you initially expected? Perhaps you understand the distinctions clearly enough, and yet you're still feeling a bit nervous or maybe overwhelmed about how effectively you'll be able to begin making some of these shifts. Does looking ahead at the path in front of you give you a sense of trepidation? Exhilaration? Some of both?

However you reacted, I congratulate you for being honest with yourself, and for having the courage to look at where you are on this path, and where you have a little — or a lot of — room to grow.

Stepping Onto the Path

Regardless of the assortment of your reactions — and I imagine that your responses were broad and varied — here are the first three steps you must take in order to step onto this path and begin your intentional journey from fear to love:

STEP #1: B — R — E — A — T — H — E

A lot of research has been done on the therapeutic advantages of breathing properly. Sounds funny, doesn't it? You'd think that we wouldn't have to think about breathing.

But there are quite a few organizations out there that have researched breathing, and use specific breathing techniques as a form of therapy.

One in particular is the OxyGenesis Institute. On their website, www.oxygenesis.org, they suggest that:

> *We are all born with the innate ability to express, or "push out," emotions (sometimes referred to as energy in motion) when they become overwhelming. Laughter, yawning, crying, and even singing, all facilitate the expression of a variety of feelings...*
>
> *As we are conditioned to live in society, however, many of these natural forms of expression are stifled and even shamed. We quickly learn that it is not acceptable to cry, for example, when we feel physical or emotional pain. In order to hold back those tears, we must constrict our breathing and disengage our mind from body and soul. The energy that was meant to move through us on a wave of breath gets trapped in our constricted muscles and is stored as tension in the subconscious mind.**

---

*Note: in granting permission to use this quote from their site, the OxyGenesis Institute requested that I also pass along this information: "Most 'conscious connected breathing' methods are used to eliminate restricted breathing patterns, by working on the subconscious level to change the reaction to stressors from 'restrict the breath' to 'expand the breath.' Unless this change is made on the subconscious level, it is nearly impossible for people to breathe and relax when under stress."

Sam

When I first read that just taking a few deep breaths could help relax my body, I started sharing that with my clients. One client, Sam, said that he felt so pressured that he didn't feel he had the time to keep stopping all day long and take deep breaths. I realized this was a powerful "coachable moment." I told him I had a digital watch that also indicated seconds. I asked him to close his eyes, and I would time him as he took five slow, deep breaths. I said "GO" and watched my watch. (This was a phone coaching session.) When he was done, I looked at my watch — one minute and six seconds. I asked him how he felt, and he reported that he felt more relaxed than he had for months. I asked him how much more he felt he could accomplish in that relaxed state — he said "a lot!" Then I asked him if he had one minute and six seconds to spare a few times a day. It was a powerful exercise. Sam made the commitment to stop and take five slow, deep breaths at the top of every hour. In our next session a week later, he reported feeling more focused and productive than he'd ever felt. All from breathing!

Don't let your fears choke your breath, and drain the Life Force out of your relationship. To move from fear to love, you must allow the fear-filled energy to move through you. So BREATHE! deeply, consciously, all day long.

STEP #2: STOP Doing What's Not Working!

The next thing you must do is to start paying attention to what you're thinking, saying, and doing that's no longer serving your highest good. You cannot change what you are not aware of. When you are more intentional about just observing yourself, you set the powerful process of conscious, personal evolution into motion.

Begin by scheduling a couple of breaks during each day — just a moment or two — to check in with yourself. Are you feeling confident? Anxious? Peaceful? Agitated? If you're feeling anxious and agitated, it's a pretty strong signal that what you're thinking and saying is NOT contributing to your best and highest good, and a loving state of inner Being.

Also begin noticing when your energy feels like it's starting to shrink, and when you feel you are withdrawing into yourself. Or notice when you are feeling defensive or aggressive toward your partner. In that moment, pay attention to what you are thinking. What words are coming out of your mouth? The next time you hear yourself thinking or saying anything resembling what was described as the Unconscious Relationship, just stop. Then take a deep breath — or two or three or ten — whatever it takes to push the pause button on your old thought and behavior patterns.

STEP #3: Make One Choice.

The very next time you have the opportunity to consciously and intentionally choose love over fear, DO IT! Shift one angry thought to one compassionate thought. Change one jealous word to one supportive word. The next time you feel yourself ready to respond in your old fear-filled way, think about how you would like to respond instead — in an evolutionary way — then do that — the best way you can in that moment.

This whole process is **not** about achieving some lofty goal of perfection — however you define that. The point is **not** to focus on being great at it, or doing it better than your partner — this is not a competition (that's an unconscious, fear-filled response). The point is to do the very best you can in each and every moment. The point is to find a way to trust that by making that first choice, the rest will follow. And regardless of how large or small that decision feels, when you also reinforce your intention with the **ACTION** of following through with your choice, your personal evolution is guaranteed.

This is what it takes to step onto the conscious, intentional path and move from fear to love: breathe; stop doing what's not working; and make one new, loving choice.

Staying On the Path

After you've made that first choice to choose love over fear, staying on the Evolutionary Relationship path is really about making the moment-by-moment commitment to string lots of small, individual choices together, one after another, after another, after another.

This process is much like hiking up a mountain: all that's required of you is to put one foot in front of the other. Just pay attention to the thoughts you are thinking right now. If your thoughts in this moment are based on fear, or anger, or jealousy, explore the best way to shift them to thoughts of love and compassion. Then do the best you can, in this moment, to choose loving thoughts over fear-filled thoughts. Then, in the next moment, pay attention to your thoughts, and make another choice to choose loving words over destructive words.

You know all the analogies and metaphors: a journey of a thousand miles begins with a single step; lots of small baby steps add up to one giant leap; and on and on and on. Well, those are all true and definitely apply here.

When you make the commitment to yourself to put one foot in front of the other, you **will** get somewhere. You **will** move forward — away from fear, and toward love.

What happens if you find yourself pulled off the path by your old conditioning? Well, when you're hiking up a mountain trail, and you find that you've inadvertently wandered off the trail, don't you usually begin looking for ways to get back ON the trail? It's the same for the Evolutionary Relationship path. If you have wandered away from compassionate thoughts and words, and into the old fear-filled state of inner Being, just find your way back to the path. There's no need to waste time and energy beating yourself up — remember to send lots of that good ol' compassion your way, too.

And what if you really work at shifting your thoughts from fear to love, and you don't feel or see any changes around you yet? If the impact of choosing a new, evolved, and loving thought seems imperceptible at first, trust that through being consistent, persistent and patient, the changes will become more and more tangible with every day that passes. And have faith that you will begin seeing concrete evidence that you're moving in the right direction. In fact, decide right now that you **will** see that evidence, and it will begin magically appearing — right before your eyes!

*"I am always doing that which I can not do,
in order that I may learn how to do it."*

– Pablo Picasso

Now You Know Too Much

As a professional coach, I've observed that almost every one of my clients has run into the same obstacle at some point. They're afraid of slipping back into old patterns or habits. They're afraid they'll backslide into that fear-filled place from which they're trying to break free. They're afraid of being drawn back to the "dark side."

And I tell each one of them essentially the same thing:

You know too much to ever go back to where you were.

I suggest to them that they will always recognize when they begin heading backwards, in the direction of their old way of Being; that they will be able to catch themselves before they get all the way back to where they were before; and that they will find a way to regain their forward momentum more quickly and efficiently.

Once my clients begin to taste the freedom they create by their willingness to choose their own path through this life, they usually report feeling a spark of exhilaration — like a powerful surge of unlimited potential has started to build momentum. And as they make one small choice after another, that momentum gets easier and easier to maintain, and their innate potential continues to expand. I've witnessed great transformations occur in a relatively short period of time — sometimes within one 50-minute coaching session.

Maria

Maria hired me because she and her husband were having some challenges in their marriage, and he'd started talking about a trial separation. In our first session together, as she started telling me her story, I could feel the intensity of her anxiety and panic from two time zones away. She was in a heightened state of fear. Everything she talked about was the potential losses and her feelings of helplessness and powerlessness. She desperately wanted to hang on to the marriage, and "talk some sense" into her husband. I stayed focused on asking her what she appreciated about her husband, what she perceived as the gifts in the marriage, and what she had control over. As she described all the value she saw in her marriage — the joy, their children — she began to reconnect with her own inner power. The shift she made was almost palpable. She acknowledged her own strength and courage, and began describing with great confidence her desire to make the best of whatever future she faced, either with her husband or on her own. She really understood that her husband's path was his to chose, and her path was hers to choose. In a 50-minute session, she went from fear and panic to confidence and inner peace — all by reconnecting with her power and willingness to choose her own path, rather that to have her path determined by outside influences.

Being on a conscious path is a process of trial and error. When you try something new, sometimes it works the way you want it to, and sometimes it doesn't. Then you learn from it and you get to make a different choice next time. Then you learn from that choice, and make a better choice beyond that. This is the evolutionary path that every living creature on the planet is traveling. In his book, **Beyond the Broken Gate** (Serenity Hill Press, 2003), Charles Graybar suggests, *"There is no* *failure except the failure to learn."* And I believe that's what we humans are here do — to explore, to learn and to evolve to a higher self-awareness and more expanded consciousness. I actually see it as a biological and spiritual imperative — we almost can't help ourselves!

> *"He who knows others is wise;*
> *he who knows himself is enlightened."*
> *–Lao Tzu*

This *IS* All About You

As I was growing up in the early 1960s, one of the most prevalent messages I remember was, *don't be selfish*. We were often taught to subjugate our own needs, and to put the needs of everyone else first. When taken at face value, without any consideration for balance and perspective, this turns into a dangerous edict — especially when the suppression of our own needs causes us to compromise or abandon our personal missions. It is then that we are reduced to a society with very little direction, purpose and passion. That's when we become a collection of unconscious drones trudging through life on emotional autopilot, hoping that tomorrow won't suck too much.

Your evolutionary process, as with ***every*** aspect of your life, is **ALL ABOUT YOU**. It's all about you discovering who you are and what you're here to do — your soul's mission.

When it comes to your unique life, you must walk your own path. You must learn from your own trials and experience the joys of your own triumphs.

I can tell you that this process continues to work for me — in ways that amaze and delight me on a daily basis. I cannot tell you if or how this process will work for you, though.

I cannot — and will not try to — talk you into walking this path. The only way you will take any first step is because **you** have some level of faith that your rewards will be greater than your risks. You are the only person in your life who can decide if this is the journey upon which you want to embark, and if you're ready to take that first step.

> "The only courage that matters is the kind that gets you from one moment to the next."
> —Mignon McLaughlin

What About My Partner?

At this point, you might be thinking, *"Well, yeah, this is all well and good, but why should I do all the work? What about getting my partner to make some of these changes, too?"*

Well, the bottom line is that you cannot make anyone think, say, or do anything they don't want to think, say, or do. We humans have to have a very compelling, personal reason to make any changes in our lives — especially changes in deeply ingrained and conditioned thought and behavior patterns. We have to be able to see a personal benefit and believe that the change will at least be worth the effort.

Remember Marjorie's story earlier? Dragging your partner along this path is an unconscious response. Inviting your partner to walk this path with you is conscious and evolutionary.

If you need your partner to go along with all this stuff, because you think your relationship happiness depends on him or her choosing this path, too, that is also an unconscious response rooted in fear.

Forcing, pushing, bribing, begging = **Unconscious**.
Sharing, modeling, inviting = **Evolutionary**.

If you want to be evolutionary about this with your partner, then you begin by focusing on yourself. You begin by shifting your own thoughts and words from fear to love, which will positively impact your actions.

Charles

Charles was a client I worked with about a year ago who, after a decade of struggling with a fear-filled, victim-based, less-than-conscious relationship with his former wife, Dana, decided to put these concepts into practice. In less than six months of sending love, compassion and gratitude to his daughter's mother —

without ever saying a word to her directly — she started shifting his responses to him. His daughter even made the observation, *"Mom's really talking nice about you — even when you're not around!"* My client wondered if shifting the energy he was sending to her helped release her from the struggle, and gave her the freedom to shift, too. He was only speculating, but what if that's really what happened? If his choice to send her love was, in any way, even a small part of her own transformation, he decided it was definitely worth it to keep doing it.

But what if you find that your partner has no interest in any of this? As I mentioned previously, you cannot beg, bribe, threaten, bully, drag, force, or coerce your partner into wanting to walk the Evolutionary Relationship path with you. He has to be willing and able to do it of his own volition. She has to want to take the risk with you — it will not work if you want it more for her than she does for herself. Otherwise, it's back to the fear-filled, unconscious relationship for you both.

If your partner really does not have any interest in joining you on this journey, then you have a choice to make. I can see three main choices:

1. You can leave the path in order to stay with your partner.
2. You can continue on the path, stay with your partner, and do your best.
3. You can continue on the path without your partner and bless her on her own path.

Can you see any other options?

You are the only one who can weigh your options and make this decision. However, I will ask you the big question I ask my coaching clients:

"What choice will be most consistent with your values and help you maintain the highest level of integrity with your purpose?"

If this is a decision in front of you, I wish you a conscious, peaceful resolution. I support you in making the best decision you can in the moment, then trusting that the outcome will serve the best and highest good of everyone involved.

The Journey from Fear to Love

> "As we let our own light shine, we unconsciously give other people permission to do the same. As we are liberated from our fear, our presence automatically liberates others."
>
> —Marianne Williamson

Watch Out for the Big BUT

Have you ever said to your partner, or has your partner ever said to you,

"I love you, but..."

"Don't take this personally, but..."

"I wish I could help you, but..."

Have you also wondered why it doesn't really feel very good to say or to hear? Well, it boils down to grammar. When the word "but" is used in a sentence, it generally means "not this, but that." The word "but" essentially dismisses whatever comes before it. There are times when it's appropriate. Most of the time, though, we use it in a way that inadvertently dismisses or invalidates our partner.

When you say, *"I love you, but you're driving me crazy,"* what your partner could actually be hearing is: *"You're behaving in a way that's unacceptable to me, and it's keeping me from loving you."*

When your partner says, *"I wish I could help, but I've got too much work to do,"* what you're likely interpreting in that is, *"My work is more important than helping you."*

Now it may be true that she's not accepting your behavior and that it **is** a condition of her ability to love you. And it may be true that his work is more important than helping you. In those cases, the word "but" is often used as a way to disguise what your partner may be really feeling, and is too uncomfortable to speak his or her truth to you. That's an unconscious and fear-filled response.

The evolutionary response would be to speak your truth to your partner in a way that acknowledges your ownership of your opinion, sets a healthy boundary, and still honors your partner's feelings and needs. Try shifting "but" to "and."

Here are some evolutionary alternatives to the examples above:

"I feel uncomfortable when you behave that way, **and** *I wanted to let you know."* Or

> *"When you do [or say] that, it really triggers a strong reaction for me, **and** it feels uncomfortable."*

In these responses, you're not demanding that your partner change because you're uncomfortable. You're taking responsibility for your own response, and you're honest with your partner about how you're feeling.

> *"I do want to help, **and** right now it's extremely important to me that I remain focused on the work that's in front of me so I don't lose my momentum. Is there a time a little later that I could help you with that?"*

In this response, you're acknowledging your willingness to help, you're being honest with your partner about your priorities, and you're negotiating her request for help.

I'm not suggesting that you eliminate the word "but" from your vocabulary. I *am* suggesting that you be conscious and aware of when it's getting ready to come out of your mouth. Stop and ask yourself if you're using it to avoid telling your truth to your partner. If so, see if "and" will fit in there better.

"What do we live for, if it is not to make life less difficult for each other?"

–George Eliot

Being the Compassionate Observer

The concept of being the Compassionate Observer first came to me when I was exploring Buddhism, its definition of compassion, and looking at how it applied to me and my life.

In their book, **The Art of Happiness: A Handbook for Living** (Riverhead Books, 1998) Dr. Howard Cutler asks His Holiness the Dalai Lama, *"Can you more clearly define what you mean by compassion?"*

The Dalai Lama replied:

"Compassion can be roughly defined in terms of a state of mind that is nonviolent, nonharming, and nonaggressive. It is a mental attitude based on the wish for others to be

free of their suffering and is associated with a sense of commitment, responsibility, and respect towards the other."

The more I read about compassion, the more it all resonated with me as a way to consciously and intentionally walk a peaceful path through this life. It felt like compassion was the cure for all the drama I kept allowing myself to get sucked into — especially in my relationships.

Then one day in a meditation, I had a flash of a vision that I was both a scientist and a lab rat — at the very same time. I could imagine myself as the scientist, dressed in a white lab coat, looking down at myself as the rat who had just responded to a particular stimulus in a way that the scientist didn't expect. And the Scientist Me said, *"Well, wasn't that an interesting choice!"*

The scientist doesn't yell at the rat, call it names, or berate it for the choice it made. The scientist is neutral and observes the situation with wonder and curiosity.

When I could step out of the emotional gunk of a situation, and see my own responses and behaviors from the perspective of a curious, neutral observer, then it was easier to generate a lot more acceptance and compassion for my own humanness. I could see myself as a creature that was doing the best she could with a given set of circumstances. I could see myself as a person who is fully capable of learning from her choices, and who has the intelligence to make progressively more conscious choices as she evolves.

And the extension of that was expanding my ability to be a Compassionate Observer of other human beings, too. It has steadily become easier and more rewarding to observe human behavior through the lens of compassion — ***really accepting*** that we are all doing the best we can in any set of circumstances. I have also come to genuinely trust that we DO learn from our mistakes, and that our "best" tomorrow can be better than our "best" today.

I invite you, then, to also take on the role of Compassionate Observer — become the scientist in the white lab coat who observes himself and the world around him with wonder and curiosity. Step out of your emotional maze and observe yourself and your partner as fallible human beings with an enormous capacity for personal growth. Pull up a chair and watch with loving amazement as you both struggle and learn, struggle and learn, and then struggle some more and learn some more.

> "You want to see a miracle?" BE the miracle."
>
> – Morgan Freeman as God
> in Bruce Almighty

Are You Peeing in Your Own Pool?

There is a unified energy within which we all exist. On the physical plane, we really do seem separate. At the quantum level, though, we are all swimming in the same "pool" of energy.

Dean Radin, Ph.D., is the laboratory director and senior scientist at the Institute for Noetic Sciences. He is the author of **The Conscious Universe** (Harper Collins, 1997) and **Entangled Minds** (Pocket Books, 2006), and he has spent decades in the lab exploring psychic phenomena as evidence of our "entanglement," as it's described in the field of quantum physics* [see page 136]. From his research he postulates that our thoughts and feelings are accessible to everyone else throughout the quantum field — which means all of us.

Pretty heavy stuff, I know. But put the science aside for a minute and think about your own experiences: when was the last time you walked into a room and could "feel" the tension? Even if no one said a word, you knew the moment you entered the room that you were walking into a bunch of unhappy people. Or have you ever been talking to someone whose words sounded nice, and yet you could feel that they didn't mean them and knew they were hiding some deeper anger or judgment? You know when someone doesn't like you. You don't always know why you know, but you know.

On the other side of the same coin, every unspoken thought you send out to another person, either positive or negative, imprints on their psychological and

---

* Quantum entanglement is a prediction of quantum theory that refers to connections between "twin" particles that may be separated by miles or even on opposite sides of a universe. Some additional resources:

http://www.biophysica.com/quantum.htm
http://plato.stanford.edu/entries/qt-entangle/
http://www.newscientist.com/article.ns?id=dn2564
http://en.wikipedia.org/wiki/Quantum_entanglement

physiological response to you, too. If you don't like him, are afraid of him, or wish him harm, it's pretty likely that he knows this and will respond to you in a similar fashion (if he is also in a fear-filled, unconscious state of Being). If you think she's bossy or arrogant and you try to cover it up with a smile and sweet words, she knows it. On some level, whether she can articulate it or not, she knows it.

So you may assume you're not affected when you think a destructive thought about another person or speak a hateful word. You may even assume that the other person isn't really hurt by it. Scientific evidence is mounting that says you're wrong — on both accounts.

When you think hateful, judgmental, caustic, or angry thoughts, you're actually releasing that negative energy into the same energy field that you occupy. Metaphorically, you're peeing in your own pool.

Not a very pretty picture, is it? Well, it's not. And it happens all over the planet all the time — YUCK! That's why it's so critically important to consciously and intentionally choose your thoughts, words and actions. Doing so not only supports your partner and your relationship, but it supports you, too, and every other human being on the planet.

Here's another twist to this part of the story: think about what happens every time you think a negative, angry, hurtful thought about yourself. Yup, you guessed it! You're not only peeing in your own pool, you're also negatively impacting those around you, too.

Why do you think there's so much crime, violence, depression, anger and destructive behaviors in cities and major metropolitan areas? High concentrations of unconscious, negative thoughts are polluting the energy pool. It takes a pretty darned clear, conscious state of inner Being to "swim" in all that gunk and not be affected by it.

If you want to wake up and walk the Evolutionary Relationship path with your partner, **you must** stop peeing in our collective energy pool.

The Journey from Fear to Love

> "Set it right. Love is the only rational act. Let it come in."
>
> – *Jack Lemmon*
> *in* Tuesdays With Morrie

Tracking Your Personal Evolution

I invite you to go back right now and read all of the Unconscious and Evolutionary Relationship distinctions again. Really look at where you are on your own journey from fear to love.

I also invite you to schedule an appointment with yourself in three months, six months and one year from today to come back to this book and re-read the Unconscious vs. Evolutionary Relationship distinctions. Rate yourself again along the continuum from fear to love. Acknowledge the distance you've already traveled and celebrate your progress. And, through the eyes of the Compassionate Observer, be aware of the path that still stretches in front of you.

Waking Up, One Choice at a Time

So, which choices are you ready to make? What small step will you take today along your own Evolutionary Relationship path?

Will you choose to respond to your partner from an unconscious, fear-filled state of Being, or will you, just this one time, speak and act from a place of compassion and love? Will you choose to think the thought that crushes and judges, or the thought that empowers? Will you choose to speak the word that belittles and berates, or the word that encourages and promotes? Will you choose the response that shuts out love, or the response that opens the door and invites love to come on in and stick around for a while?

Once you've made that first conscious choice, all it takes is to make just one more. Then one more, then one more, then one more.... I hope you get the picture.

"Kindness gives birth to kindness."
— Sophocles

My dear friend, John, has helped me appreciate the value of "bottom lining" it. So here's the bottom line:

Every thought you think, every word you speak, and every action you take is YOUR choice and YOUR responsibility — no one else's. PERIOD.

And every time you choose a kind thought over a hurtful thought, your own heart softens. Every time you choose a compassionate word over a judgmental word, you soften the heart of another. Every time you choose a loving action over a destructive action, you open the door to the possibility that others will have the courage to follow your example.

Each and every time you choose love over fear you invite a little more peace into your life and into the world.

Here is my heartfelt prayer for you:

May you choose your thoughts, words and actions carefully, consciously, and deliberately.
May you always hold love, kindness and compassion in your heart.
And may you travel the journey from fear to love with gratitude and grace.

ABOUT LAURIE

Laurie Cameron is on a mission: to be a compassionate catalyst for expanding human consciousness and an enthusiastic advocate for conscious choice. Through her speaking, writing, training and coaching, she is dedicated to wiping victim mentality off the face of the planet. She firmly believes compassion is the most effective and efficient path to world peace — from the inside out, one thought at a time.

Laurie has traveled a path of great diversity during this lifetime. She has a BS in Forestry/Outdoor Recreation from Colorado State University, and spent a handful of years working at various national forests and state parks. Before she found coaching in 1998, she spent 16 years as a drafting technician for civil and mining engineering and land surveying.

Laurie is a graduate of Coach U, a Master Certified Relationship Coach with Relationship Coaching Institute, and a Certified Coach with Coach Training

Alliance. Between being a coach for nine years, a trainer for Relationship Coaching Institute for four years, and a trainer for Coach Training Alliance for over five years, Laurie has trained and coached thousands of people worldwide. She is a contributing author for *Exploring Coaching* e-book, and is the author of *The Sage and Scholar's Guide to Coaching Singles*. Her articles have been published in numerous magazines and newspapers, and she published her own weekly e-zine, *Thriving After Divorce*, for three years.

Laurie lives in a quiet suburb of Denver, Colorado, and savors the time she gets to spend with her grown daughter and with her wonderful friends. She has a passion for hiking, nature, road trips, racquetball, good wine, baseball, singing, and traveling, and she wants to experience as much of the world as she possibly can in this lifetime.

To book Laurie for a speaking engagement, book signing, or training, contact her at: booklaurie@lauriecameron.com.

RESOURCES & READING LIST

Seven Steps to Success I Learned From Homeless People, Chet Sisk, Stratford Books, Inc., 2005

Beyond the Broken Gate: An Ordinary Man's Extraordinary Journey to Learning Who We Are, Why We Live, and Where We're Going, Charles Graybar, Serenity Hill Press, 2003

The Art of Happiness: A Handbook for Living, His Holiness the Dalai Lama and Howard C. Cutler, M.D., Riverhead Books, 1998

The Conscious Universe, Dean Radin, Ph.D., Harper Collins, 1997

Entangled Minds, Dean Radin, Ph.D., Pocket Books, 2006

The OxyGenesis Institute, www.oxygenesis.com

Additional Reading Recommendations

Loving What Is: Four Questions That Can Change Your Life, Byron Katie, Harmony Books, 2002

If the Buddha Dated: A Handbook for Finding Love on a Spiritual Path, Charlotte Kasl, Ph.D., The Penguin Group, 1999

If the Buddha Married: Creating Enduring Relationships on a Spiritual Path, Charlotte Kasl, Ph.D., The Penguin Group, 2001

You're Never Upset for the Reason You Think: The CURE for the Common Upset, Layne and Paul Cutright, Heart to Heart International, 2004

Getting the Love You Want: A Guide for Couples, Harville Hendrix, Ph.D., HarperPerennial, 1988

How Did I Get Here?: Finding Your Way to Renewed Hope and Happiness When LIfe and Love Take Unexpected Turns, Barbara DeAngelis, Ph.D., St. Martin's Press, 2005

Power vs. Force: The Hidden Determinants of Human Behavior, David R. Hawkins, M.D., Ph.D., Hay House, Inc., 2002

The Invitation, Oriah Mountain Dreamer, HarperCollins Publishers, Inc., 1999

The Power Path: The Shaman's Way to Success in Business and Life, Jose Stevens, Ph.D., New World Library, 2002

The Mastery of Love: A Practical Guide to the Art of Relationship, Don Miguel Ruiz, Amber-Allen Publishing, Inc., 1999

The Biology of Belief: Unleashing the Power of Consciousness, Matter, and Miracles, Bruce Lipton, Ph.D., Mountain of Love/Elite Books, 2005

The Power of Belief: Essential Tools for an Extraordinary Life, Ray Dodd, Hampton Roads Publishing Company, Inc., 2003

Conscious Dating: Finding the Love of Your Life in Today's World, David Steele, RCN Press, 2006

Coaching Resources

Laurie Cameron's website: www.LaurieCameron.com

Sage and Scholar's Guide for Coaching Singles: For coaches who want to add singles coaching to their business.

http://www.coachtrainingalliance.com/sage_scholars/singles_coaching.php?a_aid=019563

For the full availability of **Sage and Scholar's Guides** for other coaching specialties, go to the site link listed above.

Prosperous Coach: A content-rich membership site for coaches who want to create and maintain a financially successful and sustainable coaching business.

http://www.prosperouscoach.com/products/item23.cfm?affid=catalyst56

Working Websites for Coaches: This is an amazing resource for creating a professional coaching website.

http://www.prosperouscoach.com/products/item23.cfm?affid=catalyst56

Exploring Coaching e-book: Learn the ins and outs of becoming a professional coach from ten coaches who know

http://exploringcoaching.com

Coach Training Alliance: The best coach training for the smallest investment in the shortest time.

www.CoachTrainingAlliance.com

Relationship Coaching Institute: The first and best training and resource organization for relationship coaches.

http://www.profcs.com/app/?af=40694